RICHARD
HAMMOND'S
BLAST
LAB

DON'T

INSECTS

GET

FAT?

BLAST LAB
A September Films Production in association with Hamster's Wheel
Productions for the BBC. September Films is a division of DCD Media.

Dorling Kindersley

LONDON, NEW YORK,
MELBOURNE, MUNICH and DELHI

Ed   ox

Scier   hetti

First published in Great Britain in 2009 by
Dorling Kindersley Limited
80 Strand, London WC2 ORL

Text © 2009 Richard Hammond & September Films Limited
A division of DCD Media
Layout and design © 2009 Dorling Kindersley Limited
A Penguin Company

BBC, CBBC and the BBC and CBBC logos are trademarks of the British Broadcasting
Corporation and are used under licence. BBC logo © BBC 1996,
CBBC logo © BBC 2007

2 4 6 8 10 9 7 5 3 1

175921 – 08/09

The CIP Catalogue record for this book is available from the British Library.

ISBN: 978-1-40534-802-7

Printed and bound in England by Clays Ltd, St Ives plc

Discover more at
www.dk.com

CONTENTS

ODD BODS

Blood, guts, and funny bones

Why does your SKIN turn wrinkly in the bath?

When you're soaking in the tub, the dead outer layer of your skin absorbs water and SWELLS UP. The skin on your fingers and toes gets too BIG for what it's covering and folds into wrinkles. The same thing happens on the rest of your body, but it's not as noticeable.

Why do farts smell like rotten eggs?

Pee-yooh! That terrible trump smell comes from **CHEMICALS** in your body's waste gases. The stinkiest of those gases are sulphur compounds – which also give rotten eggs their **PONGY** smell. The more sulphur-rich foods you eat, the more smelly compounds will be made by the bacteria in your gut. Foods like cauliflower, eggs, and meat have a lot of sulphur and make really stinky farts.

Why do we get goose bumps?

A) They keep us **WARM.**

B) Goose bumps are a "danger sense" and tell us something **SCARY** is about to happen.

C) They help us sense the direction of the **WIND**.

Answer: (A) Goose bumps keep us warm by making our hairs stand up. This doesn't make much difference on humans, but it does on furry animals. Goose bumps make an animal's fur fluff up, and trap a layer of air that helps keep the animal warm.

WHY DO SCABS ITCH IF YOU'RE NOT SUPPOSED TO SCRATCH THEM?

Under the scab, **BRAND NEW SKIN** is growing. As the scab and the skin pull apart, nerves in the skin are moved around and this makes you feel an itch. The **ITCHING** means the wound is healing. If you scratch, the scab can pull away before the wound is healed and it can leave a scar.

Why do you blush when you get embarrassed?

A) IT'S CAMOUFLAGE. The red colour helps you **BLEND** in better with your surroundings.

B) So you will **STAND OUT** more so everyone will know to avoid you.

C) Your body is getting ready to **RUN AWAY**!

Answer: (C) When you're nervous or embarrassed, your body releases a chemical called adrenaline. Adrenaline makes your heart beat faster so you're ready to run from danger. It also makes more blood flow through the veins in your face, turning it red!

WHY DOES YOUR LEG FALL ASLEEP?

If you've been squashing part of your body for a long time it may feel tingly, heavy, and hard to move. The pressure on that part of your body has **SQUASHED** the nerves inside, which carry information to and from the brain. This stops some of the **NERVES** working, and makes it hard for your brain to communicate with that body part.

Can cold weather give you a cold?

Not really! The germs that cause colds don't actually **LIKE** cold weather – like us, they prefer to stay in the warm. The real reason we often catch colds in the winter is that we spend more time indoors with other people. So **GERMS** can spread more easily from person to person.

8

Why do your ears make wax? What does it do?

Greasy, yellow earwax may look pretty icky but it actually keeps your ears clean. It traps dust, dirt, and **NASTY BUGS** that could damage your hearing. It also stops your ear from drying out. Over time, old wax **HARDENS** and is pushed out of your ear by new wax. Pieces of crusty earwax can drop out when you move your jaw – for example as you talk or eat.

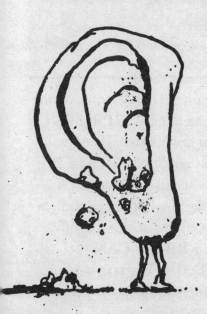

WHY DOES SPINNING AROUND MAKE YOU DIZZY?

A) Spinning makes your **BRAIN** revolve inside your skull, which makes it hard to think straight.

B) When you **SPIN FAST**, your brain can't keep up with what your eyes are seeing. This causes dizziness.

C) Your **EARS** are telling your **BRAIN** that you're still moving.

Answer: (C) Inside your ears are fluid-filled tubes that send your brain information about movement. After you stop spinning, the fluid keeps sloshing about for a while, so your brain thinks you're still moving!

Why can't you tickle yourself?

Being tickled depends on the element of **SURPRISE**. If you don't know where or how you'll be **TICKLED**, the unexpected sensations make you laugh and squirm. But if you tickle yourself, your **BRAIN CAN PREDICT** what's coming – and this makes you feel less sensitive, or ticklish.

Why do you pee more often when you're cold?

When it gets cold, your body keeps warm by sending less blood to your **SKIN** and more blood to your **ORGANS**. All this blood squeezed into the middle of your body makes your blood pressure higher. Your kidneys try to bring down your blood pressure by taking water out of it. They do this by making urine – so you pee more.

WHY DOES YOUR NOSE RUN WHEN IT'S CHILLY?

Your nose is full of blood vessels. These work with special glands to make "mucus" – **SNOT** to you and me. The blood vessels get bigger in cold weather, because warm blood flows through your nose to protect it from the cold. The extra blood flowing to your glands makes them work harder, and this means that your nose makes a lot more snot! Sniff, sniff...

Which came FIRST? The chicken or the egg?

It was the egg - and probably a DINOSAUR egg at that. Many evolutionary biologists believe that birds evolved from egg-laying dinosaurs. Dinosaurs themselves evolved from reptiles, which were the first animals to lay eggs on land.

13

How high can birds fly?

The highest a bird has ever been spotted is **11,300 m** (37,000 ft) above ground. A Rüppell's griffon vulture once hit a plane at this height – way above this vulture's usual cruising altitude. Bar-headed **GEESE** are probably the world's most regular high-flyers. These birds fly over the Himalayas at around **9,000 m** (29,500 ft). They do this to ride a strong air current called the jet stream, which helps them fly **1,600 km** (1,000 miles) in a day.

How do homing pigeons find their way home?

A) TINY MAGNETS in their heads can sense Earth's magnetic field.

B) They have **GOOD** memories and remember what places look like.

C) They track the position of the **SUN**.

Answer: (A, B, and C) Scientists are not certain how homing pigeons find their way home, but experiments have shown that they use all of these methods to navigate.

Why do birds fly to other countries?

A) They want to get a nice **TAN**.

B) There is more **FOOD** in the new country.

C) They fancy a change of **SCENERY**.

Answer: (B) Almost half of bird species migrate to another country for part of the year. This is usually to find food, which can become scarce in cold weather. Most of the species that migrate go to countries around the equator that are warm and sunny and have a good supply of food all year round. When it is time to breed, they fly home again.

CAN BIRDS FLY BACKWARDS?

Only one bird can fly backwards – the **HUMMINGBIRD**. It does this by moving its wings in a circular motion. It can also hover by beating its wings in and out in a figure-of-eight pattern. Hummingbirds can also fly **UPSIDE-DOWN**, dive at speeds of around 100 km/h (60 mph), and take off immediately at almost **FULL SPEED**.

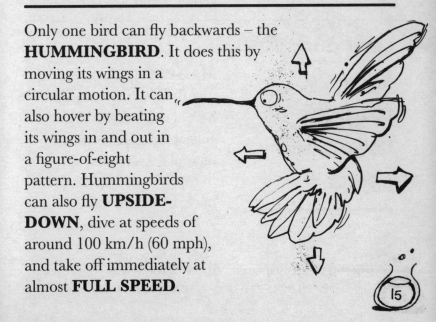

Why do parrots talk, but chickens simply cluck?

A) CHICKENS don't have anything to say.

B) PARROTS learn sounds so they can identify each other.

C) Parrots learn sounds to attract a **MATE**.

Answer: (B) Some birds, such as songbirds, parrots, and mockingbirds, have a muscly voice box that enables them to imitate sounds. For parrots, copying the call of other members of the flock may help identify the members of the group. So when your pet parrot repeats what you say, it's probably because it sees you as another member of the flock.

Why do magpies collect shiny objects?

MAGPIES, like many members of the crow family, have a natural tendency to collect and store items of food. They are also attracted to shiny objects that catch the eye, such as coins, rings, and aluminium foil. Even when the magpie discovers the item can't be eaten, it will **HIDE** it somewhere.

WHY DO MIGRATING BIRDS FLY IN FORMATION?

They do it to share the work. **FLYING** long distances is tiring because the birds have to push against the air, and this is hard work. To get a break from this, the birds fly in a **V SHAPE**. The lead bird creates a trail of **AIR TURBULENCE** that gives the birds behind extra lift, making it a little bit easier for them to fly. While **MIGRATING**, the birds take turns in the more tiring lead position.

Why do ostriches bury their heads in the sand?

A) They are looking for **FOOD** in the sand.

B) They think that if they **CAN'T SEE YOU**, you can't see them.

C) IT'S A MYTH – they don't bury their heads at all.

Answer: (C) Ostriches don't really bury their heads in the sand, but when threatened, an ostrich will fall forward and lay its head on the ground. The ostrich does this to try and fool the predator into thinking it's a bush. Because the ostrich's head and neck are sand coloured, it can look as though the ostrich is burying its head in the sand.

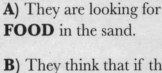

17

WHY DO PEOPLE GET HIT BY BIRD POO, BUT NEVER BIRD PEE?

You are actually getting hit by both at the same time. Bird pee is a **SEMI-SOLID**, not a liquid. Every animal builds up too much nitrogen as it eats and has to get rid of it. In humans, this extra nitrogen is turned into **UREA**. Urea dissolves in water, so we get rid of it by peeing. Birds, however, get rid of their excess nitrogen as uric acid. This doesn't dissolve in water, so bird pee is more like a **PASTE** than a liquid.

How does a baby bird breathe inside its shell?

An eggshell may seem **SOLID**, but it is covered in thousands of tiny holes. These holes let **OXYGEN** seep in and carbon dioxide (which is given off when the bird breathes out) escape. There is also an **AIR SAC** at the blunt end of the egg that slowly shrinks as the chick gets bigger.

Do penguins ever get cold?

Emperor penguins, which spend winters in the **ANTARCTIC**, do get cold, but can survive much lower temperatures than any other animal. The penguin is insulated by thick layers of fat (**BLUBBER**) and overlapping, tightly-packed feathers. In the winter, when temperatures reach −60°C (−22°F) and winds reach **200 km/h** (125 mph), the colonies of emperor penguins keep warm by huddling together.

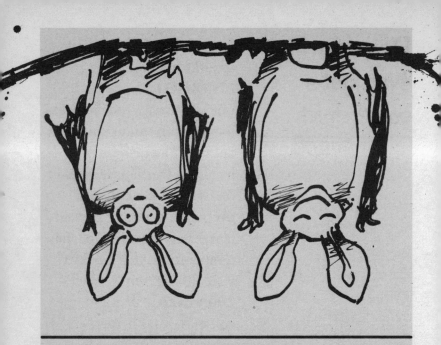

WHY DO BATS SLEEP UPSIDE DOWN?

One reason is that it puts them in the **PERFECT POSITION** for takeoff. Bats can't take off from the ground, so by hanging upside down in a tall tree or cave they are all set to **LAUNCH** in a hurry. Hanging upside down also allows bats to roost where **PREDATORS** can't reach them. It doesn't take any effort to sleep upside down either – the weight of the upper body pulls down on the tendons connected to the **TALONS** on their feet, so they lock their grip automatically. This enables them to hang in a deep sleep for weeks on end without getting cramp or falling off.

Why do flamingos turn pink?

The colour comes from the **FOOD** flamingos eat. Flamingos eat algae and millions of small **SHRIMPS**. The shrimps and algae contain chemicals called beta-carotenes that turn flamingo feathers pink. If they don't eat shrimps and algae, flamingos stay white. Beta-carotene is the same **PIGMENT** that makes carrots orange.

DO WOODPECKERS EVER GET HEADACHES?

A woodpecker slams its beak into a tree trunk around **20 TIMES** a second but never gets a headache or brain damage. How? Well, a woodpecker's brain is packed so tightly inside its skull, it hasn't any room to move around and slam into the skull. Also, the skull itself is made of **THICK SPONGY BONE** that helps absorb the impact of the blows.

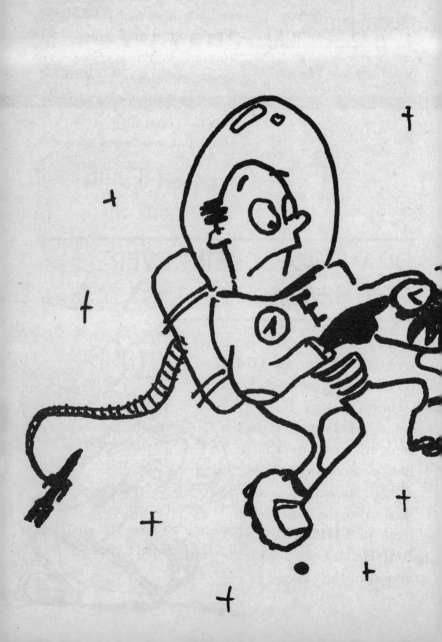

To infinity and beyond!

What TIME is it in outer SPACE?

Astronauts use Greenwich Mean Time (GMT). This is the time in London, UK, where the Greenwich Observatory is located. Or at least it is during the winter – in the summer, the UK moves an hour forward, but GMT doesn't change!

What would happen to a milk shake in space?

There's **NO AIR** in space. This is important, because it's air pressure – the push of air against objects – that normally holds liquids together. Without any air pressure, the liquid of the milk shake would fly apart into the emptiness of space. It would look like the drink had **EXPLODED** and then **VANISHED**. But the glass, which is a solid, would just float off.

WHY IS THE SUN YELLOW?

It's not really yellow at all! If you were out in space, you would see that the Sun is actually **WHITE**. The white light streaming from the Sun is made up of all the different colours of the visible spectrum – red, orange, yellow, green, blue, indigo, and violet. But as the sunlight reaches Earth, some of the blue and violet light is absorbed and scattered by gases in the **AIR**. Once you take away the blue and violet, the light coming from the Sun appears yellow.

What do spacemen eat for dinner?

A) Macaroni and cheese, scrambled eggs, tortillas – astronauts mostly eat **ORDINARY FOOD**.

B) Astronauts get all the vitamins and minerals they need from **FOOD PILLS**.

C) They only eat **FREEZE-DRIED FOOD**.

Answer: (A) These days, astronauts eat normal food, although it is packaged in special containers so it can be eaten without it flying away. Some foods are freeze dried, but not everything.

HOW DO ASTRONAUTS GO TO THE TOILET?

Very, very **CAREFULLY.** Both men and women pee using a stand-up urinal. This is made up of a funnel attached to a hose that goes to a storage unit. There's also a more normal-looking toilet – although astronauts have to strap themselves in with a seat belt to keep from floating off! The toilet uses a blast of **AIR** to push the waste into a tank.

HOW COLD IS IT IN SPACE? (SHOULD I TAKE A JUMPER?)

It's f-f-freezing. Scientists use a scale called **KELVIN** to measure the temperature in space. Zero degrees Kelvin is called absolute zero. That's the temperature at which atoms **STOP MOVING** completely. The temperature in space is about 2.725 degrees Kelvin. That's about the same as **−270 DEGREES CELSIUS**, or −455 degrees Fahrenheit.

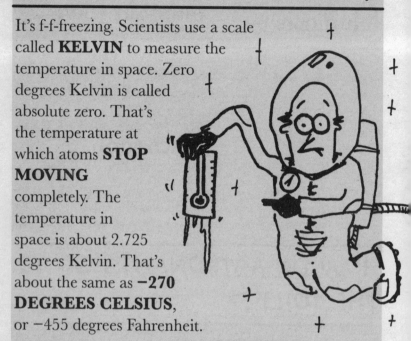

What is space made of?

NOTHING MUCH. Space has very few atoms or molecules in it – it is mostly empty **SPACE**. Some scientists believe that space may be filled with mysterious, **INVISIBLE** matter called **DARK MATTER**, but they can't detect it and don't know what it's made of.

Why don't planets bump into each other?

Well, sometimes they do – but only very rarely. Two different influences keep the planets travelling in regular orbits around the Sun. The Sun's **GRAVITY** pulls the planets towards it, but something called **MOMENTUM** is trying to push them out in a straight line. These effects balance out to make the planets travel in a curve. Very gradual changes in the planets' orbits may one day cause collisions, but not for billions of years!

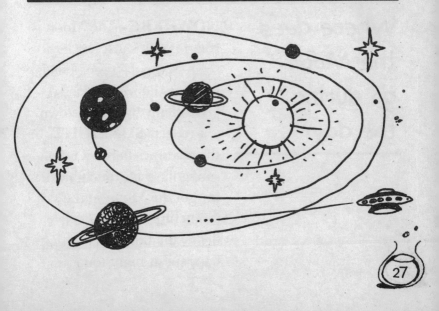

What does space sound like?

A) There's **NO SOUND** at all, because sound can't travel through the emptiness of space.

B) A STEADY HUM, like a distant vacuum cleaner. This is the sound of the vacuum of space.

C) BUZZING, clicks, and bleeps.

Answer: (A) There's no sound in space. That's because sound travels as a vibration through a material – for example air, water, or stone. Since space is mostly empty, it cannot carry sound.

Where does the Moon go during the day?

NOWHERE – the Moon is still there! It's just harder to see it in the daytime. That's because the Moon doesn't give off any light of its own – it reflects **SUNLIGHT.** In the daytime there's a lot of sunlight, so it's much harder to spot the Moon in the sky. (Sometimes the Moon is below the horizon, but that happens at night too.)

HOW BIG IS THE UNIVERSE?

Absolutely humongous. Let's imagine that you could travel as fast as a beam of light. The speed of light is about 299,792 kilometres (186,282 miles) per second – that's blisteringly fast. If you moved that fast for a year, you'd travel **9,460,528,400,000 (9.4 TRILLION) KILOMETRES** (or 5.8 trillion miles). The furthest part of the universe we know about is **46.5 BILLION LIGHT YEARS AWAY**. If you travelled at the speed of light for 46 billion years, you still wouldn't get there! And for all we know, the universe could be much, much bigger than that.

Which animals have been in space?

A) Only **MONKEYS**

B) Only **DOGS**

C) Monkeys, dogs, turtles, guinea pigs, ants, spiders, beetles, rats, cats, bullfrogs, newts, brine shrimp, bees, crickets, mice, fruit flies, snails, carp, sea urchins, guinea pigs... and **MANY MORE**!

Answer: (C) Since the first animal was launched into orbit (Laika the dog), hundreds of animals have been in space.

29

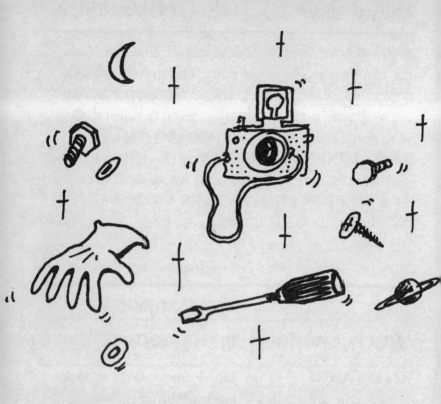

IS THERE RUBBISH IN SPACE?

LOADS OF IT. In fact, there is so much that NASA has a whole department to keep track of **SPACE JUNK**. They say there are around **17,000** objects larger than 10 cm (4 in) and around **200,000** pieces between 1 and 10 cm ($^1/_2$ in and 4 in) in diameter. The rubbish is made up of bits from old **SATELLITES,** parts of spacecraft, and the odd item dropped by astronauts – like tool bags and gloves!

What are comets' tails made of?

A) **WATER VAPOUR**, like the visible vapour trails of jet planes.

B) **DUST AND GAS.**

C) **COSMIC ENERGY**, which is propelling the comet forward.

Answer: (B) There are two types of comet tails: dust tails, and electrically-charged gas tails. Dust tails often look blue, whereas gas tails tend to look pink. Most comets have both.

WHAT ARE SHOOTING STARS?

Most shooting stars are space rocks about the size of a pebble. When they enter the Earth's atmosphere they **BURN UP**, which is why we see them as bright lights. Shooting stars range in size from a speck of sand to a boulder.

Why don't INSECTS get FAT?

Because their shells don't stretch! Insects have a hard outer shell, called an EXOSKELETON. In order to get bigger, they have to shed that shell and grow a bigger one – which is called MOULTING. Once they get to a certain size, insects stop moulting because they're full-grown adults. Some adult insects don't eat at all, and those that do eat only eat enough to live. They can't moult again, so they don't have the room in their shells to get FAT.

What is the world's speediest insect?

That depends on whether the race is **FLYING** or crawling. In a crawling race, the **AMERICAN COCKROACH** and the Australian tiger beetle both clock in at around **5.5 KM/H** (3.4 mph). As for the fastest flyer – the top contender is the dragonfly, which can reach speeds of up to 80 km/h (50 mph).

Why do silkworms make silk?

Silkworms aren't worms at all – they're actually a kind of **CATERPILLAR**! And they make silk for the same reason that all caterpillars make it – they use it to build their **COCOONS**. The silk we use to make clothes comes from the larvae of the mulberry silk moth. Their cocoons are boiled and then the silk is slowly unwound and spun into thread. Each cocoon contains about **1.6 KM (1 MILE)** of silk.

Why do insects fly in circles around light bulbs?

A) They want to **SEE** where they're going.

B) Because they think the light is the **MOON**.

C) Because they're drawn to the **WARMTH**.

Answer: (B) Some insects that come out at night navigate using the Moon as a reference point. When they see a bright light that isn't the Moon, they get very confused. As they fly past the "Moon" they try to correct their route, and this makes them fly round and round in a circle.

WHAT IS THE WORLD'S MOST DANGEROUS INSECT?

The insect with the strongest venom is a tiny ant called **POGONOMYRMEX**. This little creature can kill a rat or a rabbit with 12 stings, and a human with 350 to 450 stings. But far and away the deadliest insect is the **ANOPHELES MOSQUITO**, which carries malaria. Malaria kills between 1 million and 3 million people each year.

DO INSECTS BURP AND FART?

Some do, but you'd have to listen very closely to hear them! In humans, belches and trumps are caused by **BACTERIA** in our guts, which release methane gas. But very few insects have methane-making bacteria in their intestines. A small number of wood-eating insects, including termites, have this kind of bacteria. (They need them to digest their food.) So they're the only insects that get wind.

Why does a flyswatter have holes in it?

The flyswatter we know today was invented in 1905 by **DR SAMUEL J. CRUMBINE**, of the Kansas State Board of Health. He made the first one by stapling a piece of wire netting to a stick. The holes in the swatter are needed because a fly can sense the changes in the **AIR** caused by the movement of a solid object, like a rolled-up newspaper.

Why aren't there any giant insects?

Super-sized insects roamed the Earth **300 MILLION** years ago, so why not today? The main reason has to do with how they breathe. Instead of lungs, insects breathe through small **AIR-FILLED TUBES** that take oxygen straight to their cells. If modern insects grew to giant size, these tubes wouldn't be able to get enough oxygen to the insects' cells. However, hundreds of millions of years ago, the air had a lot **MORE OXYGEN** in it than it does today. This meant that insects could grow much bigger, yet still get enough oxygen to their cells. If you lived back then, you'd have needed a truly massive flyswatter!

Why are flies so hard to swat?

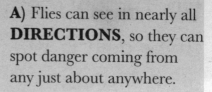

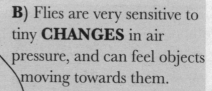

A) Flies can see in nearly all **DIRECTIONS**, so they can spot danger coming from any just about anywhere.

B) Flies are very sensitive to tiny **CHANGES** in air pressure, and can feel objects moving towards them.

C) Flies can respond to danger incredibly **FAST** – they can jump away a tenth of a second after sensing a threat.

Answer: Sorry, that was a trick question. All three answers are true!

How do glow-worms make their light?

Glow-worms can shine bright, coloured light out of their back ends. Great party trick, right? They do this by mixing up **CHEMICALS** in a special organ in their abdomen. When the chemicals are combined, they react and release **LIGHT**. Also inside the organ are **CRYSTALS** that reflect the light in the right direction.

DO TINY BUGS EVER GET SQUASHED BY RAINDROPS?

RAINDROPS don't actually crush bugs, but they can certainly knock them out of the sky. When it starts raining, larger insects can keep flying around but smaller ones find a **HIDING PLACE** as quickly as they can. Any crevice or sheltered spot will do. If they aren't fast enough, they can get **PUMMELLED ABOUT** by the rain.

How do spiders get to the top of tall buildings?

A) They **LEAP** up to the top in a single bound.

B) They make a parachute out of **SILK** and float up.

C) They **HITCH A LIFT** with a bird or a person.

Answer: (B) Many small spiders travel using a sort of silk parachute. This is called "ballooning". The spider releases a long line of silk into the wind. When the wind catches the thread, off the spider goes, riding the wind currents! The spiders have no control once they're airborne. Some end up at the top of trees, others on buildings.

What is the world's largest insect colony?

A) An ant colony **6,000** kilometres (3,600 miles) long.

B) A bee colony as big as **NEW YORK CITY**.

C) A wasp colony the size of **FOUR** football fields.

Answer: (A) Scientists have discovered a single giant colony of Argentine ants that stretches 6,000 kilometres (3,600 miles) from the Italian Riviera to northwest Spain. It's made up of billions of ants living in millions of nests that cooperate with each other.

Why are poisonous bugs brightly coloured?

A) Because the **BUGS** want predators to remember what they look like!

B) Their colour comes from the same **CHEMICALS** that make the poison.

C) Nothing's going to eat them, so they might as well **SHOW OFF** to other bugs.

Answer: (A) If predators recognize bugs as being poisonous, they won't eat them. Poisonous bugs develop striking colours and patterns so that other animals learn not to mess with them.

DO INSECTS EVER SLEEP?

Yes, they do – but the insect version of sleep is called **TORPOR**. When an insect takes a nap – or goes into torpor – most of its body functions **SLOW DOWN** and it stops moving. For example, some bees will firmly clamp on to a plant with their jaws in the evening, and let go with their legs. They then hang on like this all night, and start moving again the next morning.

Why do rubbish bins SMELL bad even when they're empty?

If a BIN isn't cleaned after being emptied, bits of damp food stay stuck inside. Bacteria multiply on the rotting food, releasing smelly gases. Plastic bins stay smelly even when clean because plastic can absorb ODOURS. Use a bin liner to stop a bin smelling.

43

WHY DOES BREAD CHANGE COLOUR IN THE TOASTER?

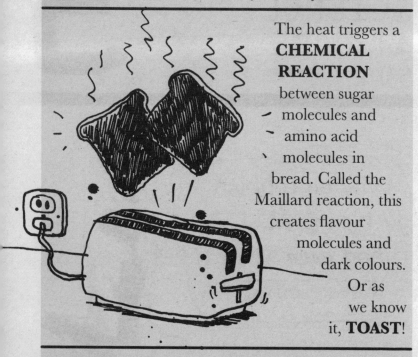

The heat triggers a **CHEMICAL REACTION** between sugar molecules and amino acid molecules in bread. Called the Maillard reaction, this creates flavour molecules and dark colours. Or as we know it, **TOAST**!

How does clingfilm cling?

Clingfilm is made mostly from **POLYTHENE**, which isn't normally sticky. To make it stickier, a chemical called (deep breath) polyisobutylene is added. This acts like a weak version of the glue on sticky tape. Being very thin also helps clingfilm to fold easily, and so stick to itself well.

The tyres on your car wear out and go bald, but where does the rubber go?

A) It **RUBS** off onto the road.

B) It goes into the **AIR**.

C) It **STICKS** to the bottom of your car.

Answer: (A) The rubber wears off onto the road as you drive because of friction between the tyre and the road. Eventually it blows off the road as dust.

WHAT IS HOUSEHOLD DUST MOSTLY MADE OF?

Dead skin cells, right? Wrong. Household dust varies enormously from place to place, house to house, and room to room. Often it's mostly fine soil or mineral particles from outdoors. There's also pollen, fungal spores, dead insect fragments, fabric fibres, hair, a small amount of human skin, and dust mites.

WHY DO DRINKS IN CARTONS POUR BETTER IF YOU POUR THEM FAST?

If you try and pour a drink from a carton too slowly, the liquid will dribble down the outside of the carton, making a mess rather than falling into your glass. This happens because an **ADHESIVE FORCE** makes water molecules stick to the carton wall. Once a trickle starts flowing down the outside of the carton, it pulls more liquid down with it thanks to a **FORCE OF ATTRACTION** between water molecules. If you pour a drink quickly, however, the water leaves the carton with so much **MOMENTUM** that it overcomes the adhesive force and heads straight into the air. Just make sure your glass is there to catch it.

Why does toast always land butter-side down?

If you drop a slice of buttered toast, the chances are that the butter (or jam) will hit the floor rather than the plain side. The reason is that falling objects slowly **ROTATE**, but your toast doesn't have time to make a whole turn. If you carried your toast at **HEAD** height, it would be more likely to land plain-side down.

Why does steam make ironing cotton clothes easier?

Cotton is made of **CELLULOSE** molecules, which in turn are made from **SUGAR** molecules joined together in very long chains. Heat softens and reshapes these chains, and the water in steam dissolves in the cellulose and helps the chains slide over each other more easily. The pressure of the iron flattens the softened chains, ironing out the wrinkles and making the fabric smoother.

WHY IS IT THAT A FOOTBALL BOUNCES BUT A PILLOW DOESN'T?

A football bounces because it stores **ENERGY** by **SQUASHING UP** like a spring when it hits the ground. As the football springs back into shape, the stored energy is released as movement energy, making the football rise. Objects that don't keep their shape this way can't store energy and so don't bounce. Think what happens when you drop a pillow on the floor, for instance. It simply **CRUMPLES** into a new shape, which stops it from bouncing. A poorly inflated football also crumples, so a football must be well inflated for maximum bounciness.

Does soap get dirty?

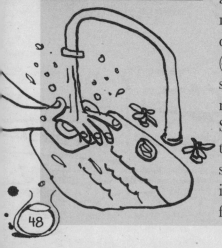

Yes, but dirty soap can still clean your hands. Particles of dirt stick to a bar of soap and stay in place until the next person uses it. The real question is whether germs (**BACTERIA**) that stick to soap can contaminate the next person's hands. Scientists have found that the **DIRT** and germs on soap wash away very easily in running water. So don't forget to rinse!

WHY DO CARS MAKE YOU FEEL CARSICK?

Travel sickness (motion sickness) occurs when you're inside a moving vehicle but not watching the world outside. Your **EYES** tell your brain that your body is still, but the sense organ inside your **EAR**, which detects movement, tells your brain that you're moving. The confusion triggers the vomiting reflex because swallowed poisons can have the same effect.

Why doesn't superglue stick to the inside of the tube?

A) TWO CHEMICALS in the tube only mix together once the tube is opened.

B) You have to say the **MAGIC** word first.

C) Superglue only becomes sticky when it is **EXPOSED** to water.

Answer: (C) Superglue actually needs a little water in order to become sticky. It's packed into the tube without any moisture, but once it comes out, the water vapour in air is enough to activate it.

What electrical appliance in my house uses the most energy?

Refrigerators use the most **ENERGY** altogether because they're on 24 hours a day (though the heat pump comes on intermittently). Clothes driers and washing machines use more energy per second (more **POWER**) but aren't on all day.

Where did people get ice before refrigerators?

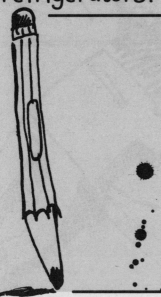

A) From deep **UNDERGROUND**.

B) They **STORED IT** from winter in warehouses.

C) They cut it out of **ARCTIC GLACIERS** and shipped it around the world.

Answer: (B) Before refrigeration, people who lived in cold places sometimes stored ice, packed in sawdust, in insulated houses. The ice would last several months this way. Some people had ice delivered to their homes from commercial ice houses, and some ice was imported from abroad. But mostly, people did without ice. Drinks could be cooled by keeping them in water or leaving them outdoors.

DO PENCILS HAVE LEAD IN THEM?

No. Pencil lead is not lead at all – it's a combination of **CLAY** and the mineral **GRAPHITE**. These are finely ground, mixed together with water, and then compressed at high temperatures to make **THIN RODS**. We call it lead because the people who first discovered that graphite was handy for writing thought it was a black form of lead.

SEEMS A BIT FISHY

Tall tales of life underwater

Why do some SHARKS go to the DENTIST?

Sharks have a lot of SHARP pointy teeth and these teeth tend to get bits of food stuck between them. To take care of this problem, sharks let small fish, called CLEANER FISH, swim into their mouths and eat the bits of food stuck there. The cleaner fish get a meal and the shark gets clean teeth. The sharks return the favour by not eating the cleaner fish.

WHAT'S SO SHOCKING ABOUT ELECTRIC EELS?

They can zap you without any need for **BATTERIES**. The electric eel makes electricity in three pairs of special organs. These organs contain cells that store **ELECTRIC CHARGE**, which the eel uses to stun prey. Big eels can deliver a burst of 600 volts, which is enough to knock a **HORSE** off its feet. They also use a smaller charge of 10 volts to navigate their way through muddy rivers and locate prey.

Can piranhas really eat a cow in a few minutes?

They certainly can, but it takes **HUNDREDS** of piranhas to eat a cow this fast. Piranhas usually hang out in schools of about 20, so it's unusual to see this many in one place. Also, feeding **FRENZIES** only happen when piranhas are starving, which is rare. In fact, they prefer prey that is already dead and a bit rotten.

Do fish drink water?

Only fish that live in the ... actively **DRINK** water. ... salty seawater sucks moistu... out of their bodies, so they have to drink to replace it. They also have special cells in their **GILLS** that filter the salt out of seawater. Freshwater fish have the opposite problem. They absorb water into their bodies in a process called osmosis. To get rid of the excess water, the fish do what we do – pee it out.

HOW DO SALMON FIND THEIR WAY BACK TO WHERE THEY WERE BORN?

Scientists have only a rough idea of how salmon find their way **HOME**. They believe the fish use **CLUES** to find the correct river mouth – including the length of day, the Sun's position and its angle in the sky, **WATER SALINITY** (saltiness), and temperature. But scientists do know how they navigate after they find the right river mouth – smell. Experiments have shown that salmon can remember the **SMELL** of the stream in which they were born.

Why don't goldfish bump into the side of the bowl?

A) Because they can **SENSE** it's there with a special organ.

B) They can **SEE** the side of the bowl.

C) They can **HEAR** you talking about it.

Answer: (A) Fish have a sense organ called a lateral line running along both sides of their body. It is used to sense changes in pressure. As the fish swims through the water, it pushes some water in front of it. The lateral line detects whether this little wave of water has bounced off something like the side of the bowl or another fish.

> What's the best way to get rid of a jellyfish sting?

A) **PEE** on it.

B) Pour **VINEGAR** on it.

C) Pour fresh **WATER** on it.

Answer: (B) Many people think urine is the best cure, but this will only sting and make you smell of pee. Doctors suggest that you carefully lift off any bits of tentacle with a stick, then soak the area in vinegar or seawater to stop the stinging cells from releasing toxins into your skin. Finally, apply a paste of baking soda to the area and scrape with a credit card to remove any stingers that are still stuck in the skin.

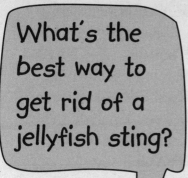

WHY DO WHALES SING?

Singing is the whales' way of making a phone call. Because whales are so large, they don't usually gather in groups (it is hard enough for one whale to find enough food), so they need some way to communicate with other whales. Sound works well because it can travel for very long **DISTANCES** underwater. Marine biologists think the songs may identify each whale, and may also give information about the whale's **HEALTH** and location.

Can fish smell underwater?

THEY CAN, although not in the same way that we do. Fish nostrils, called **NARES**, open into a chamber lined with sensory pads. As water moves over the pads, they pick up **CHEMICAL SIGNALS**. If the chemicals signal food, the fish will pursue the food; if the chemicals signal **DANGER**, it will flee.

Why are fish slippery?

A) TO ESCAPE from predators.

B) To make them **BETTER** swimmers.

C) Because they're **WET.**

CAN FLYING FISH REALLY FLY?

Yes, they can glide for short distances. The flying fish gets airborne by swimming **VERY FAST** near the water surface. Then the fish comes to the surface, spreads its large front **FINS**, and holds them rigid. The fins act like the **WINGS** of a glider – they lift the fish into the air and keep it there as it goes **SAILING** over the waves. Flying fish can stay in the air for several **HUNDRED** metres.

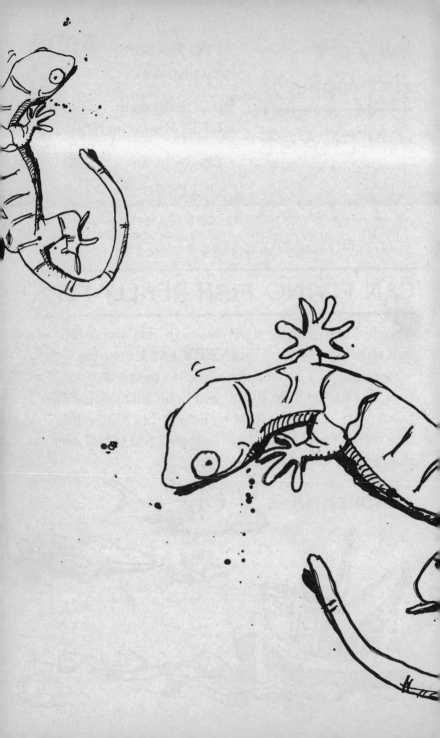

How do geckos
WALK on
the CEILING?

Geckos stick to things because
they have hairy toes. Forces
called VAN DER WAALS' forces,
which help molecules stick
together, pull the molecules in the
geckos' toe hairs towards the
molecules in the wall. Although
this force is very, very tiny,
geckos have MILLIONS of hairs
on each toe, and the combined
force is enough to prevent the
gecko falling off the ceiling.

DO ANY ANIMALS HAVE GREEN FUR?

No, but a sloth's fur often turns green because of the **ALGAE** that grow on it. The green colour helps camouflage the sloth, and the algae provide food for animals living on the sloth's fur, such as beetles and sloth moths. The bugs are attracted to the **EASY MEAL** of algae, but they also eat parasites that live on the slow-moving sloth and make it ill.

What is the most poisonous creature on Earth?

The most venomous animal on land is the **TAIPAN SNAKE**. But the deadliest creatures on the planet are box jellyfish, which can cause death within a few minutes of stinging.

Why do bulls hate red rags?

A) Bulls **HATE** all rags.

B) The colour red **ANGERS** the bull.

C) Bulls don't like being **WAVED** at.

DO MICE REALLY LIKE CHEESE MORE THAN OTHER TYPES OF FOOD?

Mice will eat just about **ANYTHING** that is vaguely nutritious. Cartoons show mice eating cheese all the time, but in reality mice prefer **GRAINS AND FRUIT**. The cheese myth came about because people found it stuck to mousetraps more easily than drier foods. A mouse wouldn't turn its nose up at cheese, but **CHOCOLATE** is more effective in mousetraps,

WHAT HAPPENS IF A POISONOUS SNAKE BITES ITSELF BY MISTAKE?

It feels the bite, but it doesn't poison itself. This is because snakes can **CONTROL** whether venom is injected or not when biting. Also, all poisonous snakes have an **ANTIDOTE** to their own venom in their blood. Everything the snake eats has been injected with its venom (it actually helps them digest food) so it obviously needs to be immune to the effects of swallowing it.

Why do wet dogs smell bad?

A) The **WATER** washes off their deodorant.

B) Oils on their **FUR** react with water to smell bad.

C) Wet fur **ABSORBS** smells from the water.

Answer: **(B)** Not all dogs smell bad when they're wet, but others are real stinkers. Most water dogs, such as retrievers, have a lot of oil glands in their skin. The oils coat the dog's fur and act as natural waterproofers, keeping the dog warm and helping it dry faster. These oils tend to have a strong smell when they get wet.

Why do falling cats always land on their feet?

In fact, falling cats do not always land on their feet and you should never drop a cat from any height. But cats can right themselves in **MIDAIR** thanks to a tiny organ in their **INNER EAR**. This organ gives the cat an idea of where its body is in relation to the ground. Because of this, the cat can **TWIST** its body while falling so that it lands on all four limbs. This absorbs the shock and helps **PREVENT INJURY**. But the cat needs to have time to turn around. Falls from a low height are safe, and falls from higher up allow the cat time to turn, but falls from a **MID-DISTANCE** are actually the most dangerous.

MEEEOWW!

DO ALL ANIMALS SLEEP?

Reptiles, birds, and mammals all sleep. Some fish and amphibians simply become **LESS AWARE** of their surroundings, but they never lose consciousness like mammals. Insects do not appear to sleep, but they do **SLOW DOWN** or become inactive for part of the day or night. Mammals that live in the sea do sleep – but only **HALF** of their brain shuts off at a time, because they need to come to the surface to breathe.

If moles are blind, how do they know where they are going?

A) They use mice as **GUIDE DOGS.**

B) They can **SMELL** their way.

C) They use the sense of **TOUCH** to guide them.

Answer: (C) A mole has a well-developed sense of touch that makes up for its poor eyesight. The tip of a mole's snout is covered in tiny bumps that respond to every object it touches. Its sensitive whiskers and body hair also help to guide the mole through the darkness of its underground tunnels.

Why do dogs walk in a circle before they lie down?

A) They like to wake up facing **NORTH**.

B) To check for **SNAKES** and bugs.

C) It **HELPS** the dog to curl up.

Answer: (B) Your dog is following its natural instincts. Wild dogs sleep outdoors, so walking in a circle is a good way to check if there are any bugs, snakes, or other dangerous things hiding in the grass. Circling may also be a way for dogs to mark their territory.

ARE ZEBRAS WHITE WITH BLACK STRIPES, OR BLACK WITH WHITE STRIPES?

Most zebras have **DARK SKIN** underneath their hair, so you can think of them as **BLACK WITH WHITE** stripes. It's the hair that carries the colour. The white stripes are simply areas where the hairs have no pigmentation.

TECHNO FILES
Geeky, freaky knowledge

What's the world's FASTEST vehicle?

That may depend on your definition of "world". The fastest vehicle is the SPACE SHUTTLE. In orbit, the shuttle reaches a speed of about 28,150 km/h (17,500 mph). During takeoff it reaches speeds of 4,970 km/h (3,100 mph). The X-15 rocket-powered aircraft, which was flown in the 1990s, reached a speed of 7,273 km/h (4,519 mph). The plane was technically in orbit when it achieved this speed, so it may also count as a space vehicle. On land, the fastest speed achieved was 1,228 km/h (763 mph) in the Thrust SSC, a twin turbofan-powered car.

HOW DOES A CAR AIRBAG KNOW WHEN TO INFLATE?

A device called a **SENSOR** tells the bag when to inflate. When the sensor detects a strong **COLLISION** force it flips a switch and the bag inflates.

Yes, but you need to hold the salt and ketchup. Fuels that are made of plant material are called biofuels, and many cars can run on them. Before the chip fat can be used in a car it has to be put through a series of chemical reactions. Plant oil, like corn oil or sunflower oil, is commonly used to make biofuel, but any type of fat or oil can be used.

Can you really run a car on chip fat instead of petrol?

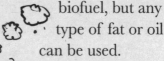

How does a car's satnav know where you are?

A) It has a **HOMING** device in the dashboard.

B) It connects with **CAMERAS** that follow your movement.

C) It uses **SATELLITES** to plot your position.

Answer: (C) Satnavs use a system of satellites, called Global Positioning Satellites, that orbit Earth. The satnav receiver locks onto signals from one or more of the satellites so it can calculate the car's longitude, latitude, and height above sea level. Software in the satnav then compares these details with a standard road map to tell you exactly where you are.

WHAT IS THE FASTEST COMPUTER IN THE WORLD?

It's the Sequoia supercomputer, currently being built for the US Department of Energy's nuclear agency. When it goes fully online in 2012 it will be capable of carrying out 20 quadrillion operations a second. Sequoia is so fast it would take the collective efforts of every person on Earth working non-stop on hand calculators 320 years to do the same calculation Sequoia can do in an hour.

Where is the internet?

A) In the **PHONE LINES**.

B) It's in a huge building in **AMERICA**.

C) It's anywhere you can **PLUG** a computer into a **NETWORK**.

Answer: (C) When your computer connects to the internet it becomes part of a local network, which is connected to millions of other networks. Information moves between networks using routers. These are large computers that manage the flow of information "traffic" – they send messages on the most direct route through the networks without jamming everyone else's computer.

HOW MANY COLOURS ARE ON A TV SCREEN?

Actually, televisions only use three colours: red, blue, and green, to produce a picture. These are arranged as a series of dots or pixels that light up when activated by a signal. When different colours of light are mixed they produce other colours: red and green gives yellow, red and blue gives magenta. Because the dots are so small and flash on and off quickly, the brain is fooled into thinking it sees all these other colours.

If computers can beat humans at chess, does that mean they are smarter than us?

Computers can't **THINK** for themselves, so they can't be smarter than humans. They can easily beat people at chess because they've been programmed to compare all the possible consequences of their next move at lightning speed and choose the one most likely to lead to a checkmate. But they don't understand why they're doing it.

WHY DOESN'T THE AIR IN A MICROWAVE OVEN GET HOT?

Microwave ovens use **MICROWAVES,** a type of invisible light energy, to cook. Certain types of microwaves are absorbed by the water, fats, and sugars in food, but not by the air around it. The microwaves make the molecules in the food vibrate, which produces **HEAT**. So, the food gets hot but the air does not.

How do they get electricity into batteries?

A) It is made **INSIDE** the battery using chemicals.

B) A special machine **PACKS** electricity into the battery at a factory.

C) It is beamed in by laser.

Answer: (A) In an ordinary battery, electricity is made using chemicals that react to produce electrons. When a battery is connected in a circuit, electrons flow out of the negative terminal and around the circuit towards the positive terminal. This movement of electrons is electricity. It is always in the battery, but only starts flowing once you connect it up.

How would a solar-powered car run when it's cloudy?

A) It wouldn't **RUN**, it would stop.

B) Using stored **ENERGY**.

C) You would have to push.

HOW DO THEY GET THE MUSIC ONTO A CD?

A CD is made by recording information as a series of bumps on a thin layer of aluminium and sandwiching it between two layers of plastic. These **BUMPS** represent the music. Inside the CD player is a **LASER**. As the laser light reflects off the bumps, the CD player converts it into an electrical signal that is then turned into sound.

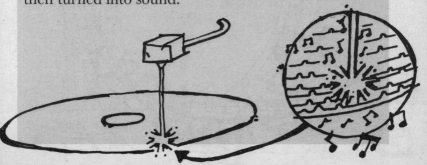

Why doesn't everyone fall out when a roller coaster loops-the-loop?

On a roller coaster, forces are acting on your **BODY** all the time. Gravity is always pulling down, but **INERTIA** keeps your body moving forward and pushes you down into your seat. You pass through the top of the loop so quickly you momentarily feel like you're falling out but you are pulled forwards by the downwards acceleration so quickly that it doesn't happen. The safety harness is for **EXTRA** security, but in most loop-the-loops, you would stay in the car without one.

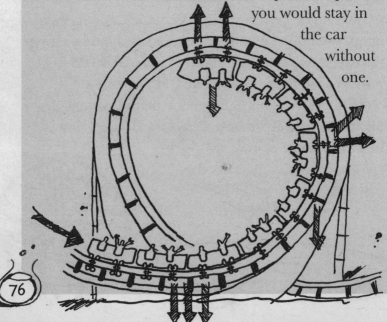

Why do people sometimes have red eyes in photos?

The spooky red-eye effect happens when **LIGHT** from a camera flash reflects off the **RETINAS** at the back of the eyes. The red colour you see comes from the **BLOOD VESSELS** that supply the retina.

HOW HIGH CAN YOU BUILD A SKYSCRAPER?

No one knows. Many things limit the height of skyscrapers, but engineers are finding new ways around these problems all the time, so skyscrapers keep getting taller. **WEIGHT** and sway are two big problems. The higher you go, the stronger the lower floors have to be to support the weight of the upper floors. Today, most skyscrapers have a strong central core that takes the pressure so the outer walls need only support their own weight. The Citicorp Center in New York uses a giant pendulum to counteract any sway on the building caused by high winds.

FLOWER POWER

Give plants a try – they could grow on you...

9

What's the world's BIGGEST flower?

The corpse flower (Rafflesia arnoldii) is a very rare plant found in the rainforests of Indonesia. It has no roots, stem, or leaves of its own. This is because it's a PARASITE, and takes all its water and nutrients from a vine root. A corpse flower can grow to be nearly a metre (three feet) across. That's as wide as a four-year-old child is tall! Its chunky PETALS are about 2 cm (0.8 in) thick. And at 10 kg (22 lbs), it weighs more than the biggest bowling ball.

WHAT ARE THE WORLD'S BIGGEST SEEDS?

SEYCHELLES COCONUTS look like two normal coconuts joined together. These fruits from the Seychelles islands in the Indian Ocean take up to **TEN** years to grow. By the time one falls from a tree, it can be up to 45 cm (18 in) long and weigh 18 kg (40 lbs). Never, ever sunbathe under a Seychelles coconut tree!

Do plants ever eat animals?

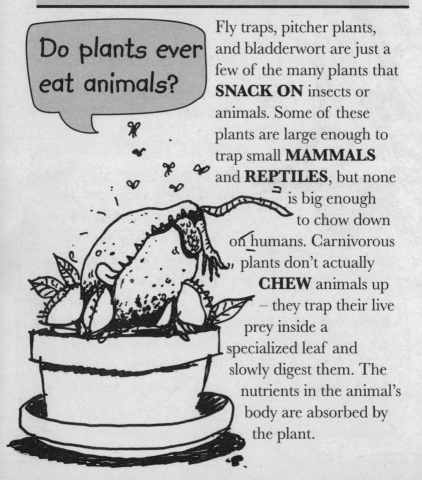

Fly traps, pitcher plants, and bladderwort are just a few of the many plants that **SNACK ON** insects or animals. Some of these plants are large enough to trap small **MAMMALS** and **REPTILES**, but none is big enough to chow down on humans. Carnivorous plants don't actually **CHEW** animals up – they trap their live prey inside a specialized leaf and slowly digest them. The nutrients in the animal's body are absorbed by the plant.

WHAT'S THE WORLD'S PONGIEST FLOWER?

The world's largest flower is also one of the **STINKIEST** blooms. A corpse flower gives off a truly revolting smell, like rotting meat. This horrible stench attracts insects that pollinate the plant. But the worst smelling plant of all is the **TITAN ARUM**. This plant only blooms for a couple of days every few years, but when it does, it smells like a dead elephant!

Corpse flower

Where do pineapples grow?

A) On **TREES**.

B) On **BUSHES**.

C) Out of the **TOP** of another pineapple.

Answer: (C) If you plant the green, leafy part of a pineapple a stalk will grow from it ending with another fruit! First you twist the leafy top off a pineapple and remove the sweet flesh — but leave the little round structures. Let this part of the pineapple dry out for about a week, then plant it in a pot full of soil.

How old is the oldest plant?

A) 80,000 YEARS.

B) 100 YEARS.

C) 1,000 YEARS.

Answer: (A) The world's oldest plant is probably a quaking aspen tree. Quaking aspens reproduce by sending out roots that pop up elsewhere and grow into new aspen tree stems. They look like separate trees but are actually branches of the main plant. There is a quaking aspen in Utah that is thought to be 80,000 years old.

WHY ARE CARROTS ORANGE?

Carrots didn't used to be orange. In fact, the first carrots, from **AFGHANISTAN**, were **PURPLE** or **YELLOW**. The original orange carrots were bred by farmers in the **NETHERLANDS** in the **17TH CENTURY**. Their bright colour was a symbol of the Dutch ruling family, called the House of Orange. The chemicals that gives modern carrots their colour are called **CAROTENES**. Carrots can also be red or white.

What's the world's most dangerous plant?

That depends on what you mean by dangerous. The plant that has killed the most people is almost certainly **TOBACCO**. But the tobacco plant isn't dangerous unless you smoke its leaves in cigarettes. Nobody knows for certain what the world's most **POISONOUS** plant is but it could be the **MACHINEEL TREE**. Every part of this tree is highly poisonous, including its sweet-smelling, tasty fruit. Just touching the tree can make your skin swell up and turn numb. Even drops of water running off its **BRANCHES** during a rainstorm can give you a blister!

WHY DO LEAVES CHANGE COLOUR IN THE AUTUMN?

A chemical called **CHLOROPHYLL** is what gives plants their green colour. Chlorophyll absorbs light – and this light is the energy that plants use to make their food. During winter, there's not as much light about, so the green chlorophyll **DISAPPEARS** from leaves and we can see other colours – reds, yellows, oranges, and browns. These are the colours that were in the leaves all along, but which were **HIDDEN** by the green chlorophyll.

Why do jumping beans jump?

A) The beans jump when tiny **INSECTS** inside them move about.

B) The beans pop like **POPCORN** as they cook in the heat of the day.

C) They jump up and down to keep **WARM**.

Answer: (A) Mexican jumping beans are actually seeds with moth larvae inside. An adult trap moth cuts a small trap door in a seed, and lays an egg inside. After the egg has hatched, the larva eats the inside of the seed. Larvae can live inside the seeds for years. When it gets too hot, the larvae move about, making the seed jump. The larva is trying to move the seed into the shade, so it doesn't dry out.

Are there any plants that travel from place to place?

At least one does. The resurrection plant acts just like any other plant when there's enough water around. But when water is scarce, the plant pulls up its roots and dries up, becoming a ball of tumbleweed. The ball is blown along by the wind until it finds water – then it sinks its roots into the wet ground, and begins to grow again.

CAN PLANTS GROW IN SPACE?

Plants can and do grow on the International Space Station and on some space shuttle flights. But without **GRAVITY**, plants grow in a chaotic, disorganized way. Scientists hope that someday we could use **PLANTS** to supply space stations with oxygen.

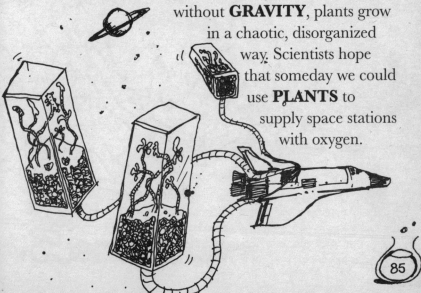

WHATEVER THE WEATHER

Weird weather wonders

10

Does lightning ever STRIKE the same place twice?

If it didn't, lightning rods would be a bit pointless. Lightning strikes some places much more often than others, such as tall buildings and trees. The Empire State Building is struck by lightning an average of 23 TIMES A YEAR and was once struck 8 times in just 24 minutes. Even people can be struck more than once. Roy Sullivan, a US park ranger, earned a place in the *Guinness Book of Records* after surviving 7 LIGHTNING STRIKES in 35 years.

CAN HAILSTONES HURT YOU?

Get out your concrete umbrella because large hailstones not only hurt people – they occasionally **KILL** by causing fatal head injuries. Hail forms in thunderstorms, but only the most powerful storms create the violent updrafts needed to hold **GIANT HAIL** aloft as it grows. In the USA, supercell storms create golfball-sized hail that wrecks cars and crops. The biggest stone on record, found in Nebraska, USA, was 18 cm (7 in) wide.

Why are rain clouds darker than other clouds?

Clouds look dark when they **BLOCK** sunlight, casting a shadow on the ground. Rain clouds block out more light than other types of cloud because they hold **MORE WATER** and are often **TALLER**. Darkest of all are stormclouds, which cast such deep shadows they make it seem like night is falling.

88

What are rainbows made of?

A) GASES in the air.

B) LIGHT hitting water in the air.

C) COLOURED DUST in the air.

Answer: (B) A rainbow forms when bright sunlight shines directly onto rain. As light passes through a raindrop, the water makes it bend. White sunlight is a mixture of different colours, and each colour bends by a different amount. As a result, the rain separates out the white light into coloured bands, forming the rainbow.

WHAT HAPPENS TO FISH IF LIGHTNING STRIKES WATER?

Fried fish. Lightning doesn't actually strike water as often as land, but water is a **GOOD CONDUCTOR** of electricity, so the electrical energy from a lightning strike can spread out as far as 30 metres (100 feet). Any fish in the immediate area would be killed.

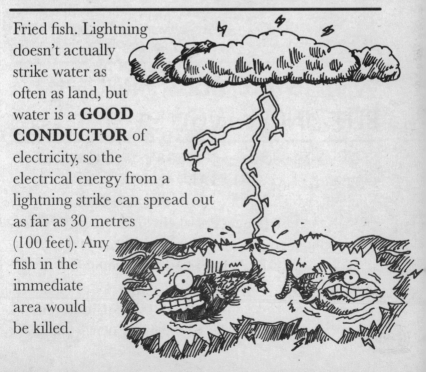

How do igloos keep you warm if they're made of ice?

A) The people living in them have **HEATERS** to warm them up.

B) The snow bricks provide very good **INSULATION.**

C) Building an igloo is such hard work it keeps you warm.

Answer: (B) Air trapped in the snow makes it a very good insulator, so any heat inside the igloo stays there. Inside the igloo is a raised sleeping platform that's higher than the entrance. Because warm air rises and cool air sinks, the raised sleeping area holds the warmth generated by a stove, lamp, or body heat. Some Inuit line their igloos with fur. The temperature inside can reach 16–20°C (60–68°F).

WHY IS ICE SEE-THROUGH BUT SNOW WHITE?

Snow is white because it's **MESSY**. It's a jumble of thousands of ice **CRYSTALS** mixed up with air. Sunlight, which is white, passes through the ice crystals but also bounces off their surfaces and so gets reflected in all directions. As a result, snow is white. Ice is solid **FROZEN WATER**. Some sunlight bounces off each surface, but most passes through, so ice is clear. Break up ice into a powder, however, and it turns white due to the many new surfaces.

When it's raining, is it better to walk or run?

This may seem like an easy question, but it is one that scientists have pondered for a long time. Not surprisingly, they **DON'T AGREE** on the answer. Some argue that running gets you **WETTER** than walking because you get pelted with rain from above **AND** in front. Other scientists reckon that because walking is slower, you'll be in the rain for **LONGER** and will get wetter. Why not give it a try?

IS IT TRUE THAT EVERY SNOWFLAKE IS UNIQUE?

To prove every snowflake is unique, you'd have to collect every one that's ever fallen and compare them – which is clearly **IMPOSSIBLE**, so nobody can say for *certain* they're all different. But it's very likely to be true. Snowflakes start as tiny six-sided **CRYSTALS**. As they fall, new crystals grow on the sides as branches (and branches grow on the branches). The form each crystal takes depends on the exact **TEMPERATURE**: they can be plates, needles, columns, ferns... Because the temperature of the air keeps changing, every snowflake develops in a unique way, and the chance of two being identical is stupendously tiny.

Why do weather reporters always get it wrong?

A) They like to watch people going out in the rain improperly dressed.

B) They're just guessing.

C) Weather reports aren't perfect.

Answer: (C) Meteorologists (weather scientists) can't make perfect forecasts. They can say what kind of weather is *most likely*, but they're never 100% certain. And the further ahead the forecast is, the greater the uncertainty.

CAN IT RAIN FROGS?

Yes, and fish as well. When a **TORNADO** forms over water, it's called a waterspout. A waterspout can suck up water containing small animals and carry them off, before dumping them miles away. If it has picked up a lot of frogs, you get frog rain. Fish, frogs, jellyfish, worms, and lizards have all been known to fall from the sky after being sucked up by a waterspout.

Can hurricanes and tornadoes really lift houses?

They don't so much lift the house as **DESTROY** it. While tornadoes and hurricanes can lift mobile homes, they can't lift houses anchored to the ground. But the abnormally **LOW AIR PRESSURE** in a violent storm can make windows explode outwards, roofs lift off, and walls collapse. Houses also get battered by **FLYING DEBRIS** picked up by the high winds.

What is the coldest place on Earth?

Officially, the coldest place on Earth is Vostock Station in **ANTARCTICA**, where the temperature reached a record low of **−89°C** (−128°F) on 21 July 1983 (and that's before adding wind chill). But there may be even **COLDER PLACES** in Antarctica where scientists have never taken a thermometer. Average winter temperatures there are around −80°C (−112°F).

WHY IS IT ALWAYS WINDY BY THE SEA?

Land warms up faster than the sea on a sunny day, causing warm air over the land to rise. This updraft sucks in air from the sea, causing a "sea breeze". The breeze is all the more noticeable because the sea is very flat, with no **OBSTACLES** to block wind.

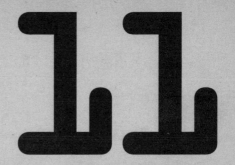

Could you REALLY travel through the jungle by SWINGING on vines?

Yes and no. Lianas are high-climbing, woody vines found in the tropics and are strong enough to support the weight of a person. But there are some problems. Lianas are PLANTS, with roots in the ground. If the liana is firmly wrapped around the upper part of the tree you can probably swing on it. If not, you'll come down to Earth with a BUMP. Always test it first. Also, the rainforest is a crowded place and there's a strong possibility you'll CRASH straight into a tree.

How can people lie on a bed of nails without getting hurt?

A) The nails are **BLUNT**.

B) They have **VERY TOUGH** skin.

C) The nails don't **BREAK** the skin as there isn't enough pressure.

Answer: (C) Pressure is the amount of force pressing on a particular area. If the force is spread over a wider area, there is less pressure on any one point. A bed of nails has lots of points that are close together, and a person lying on a bed of nails doesn't push hard enough on any one nail for it to break the skin.

HOW DO PEOPLE FIRE-WALK WITHOUT GETTING BURNED?

People really can walk over hot coals without getting burned, but it has to be done a certain way, so don't try it at home. The fire is lit well ahead of time to allow the wood to burn down to **NON-FLAMING** coals covered in **ASH**. The ash acts as an insulator. Fire-walkers don't run, but they don't dawdle either. They move quickly so there isn't time for the **HEAT** to transfer from the **COAL**, through the ash to their feet.

How does a karate expert chop through bricks with his hand?

Karate experts work on the principle that by minimizing the area of contact with which you hit something you can exert a **MAXIMUM** amount of force, so they use the side of their **HAND**, fingertips, or toes to break bricks and boards. They use softer materials to practice, but the key to a good chop is to resist the impulse to draw back at the last minute.

HOW DO ASTRONAUTS EXERCISE IN ZERO GRAVITY?

In space, exercise is not only important, it is necessary. Living in space makes bones grow **THINNER** and muscles grow **WEAKER**. On the space station, there are several exercise machines. The treadmill is a normal treadmill, but the astronauts have to wear a **HARNESS** to attach themselves to it. There is also an exercise bike that is bolted to the floor. Astronauts strap their shoes into **BUCKLES** and wear seat belts to hold themselves down. And they can use a weight-lifting device that simulates gravity.

How do people swallow swords without getting hurt?

A) By practicing **MUSCLE CONTROL.**

B) By using a **TRICK** sword.

C) They've got **IRON-PLATED** guts.

Answer: (A) Although a sword is straight and hard, and your gastrointestinal tract is curvy and soft, it is possible to learn to swallow a sword (never, ever try this at home). Sword swallowers learn to control muscles that are normally not under our control. They also train themselves to ignore the gag reflex and other discomforts.

100

When you're back on solid ground after sailing, why does everything seem to be moving up & down?

A) Because the **WORLD** is moving and it's the sea that is steady.

B) Your body gets used to **CONSTANT** movement.

C) Because you're moving too **FAST**.

Answer: (B) At sea your eyes, muscles, and inner ears sense that the water is moving up and down and send messages about it to your brain. Your body eventually gets used to the movement and the brain ignores the signals. When you return to land, your body carries on anticipating the ship's motion. This conflicts with the messages telling your brain you're not moving up and down, so you get a reverse seasickness.

DO FIRE-EATERS EVER BURN THEIR MOUTHS?

Not if they have plenty of spit, but this is not something you should try at home. Fire-eaters use fuels that burn at **LOW TEMPERATURES**. The fuel sits on top of the spit, which gives some protection to the mouth. Fire-eaters also spend hours practicing breath and **MUSCLE** control.

Do astronauts ever get "space sick"?

About half of all astronauts get space sickness during the first few days of their voyage. Inside our ears are fluid-filled structures called semicircular canals that tell us which **DIRECTION** is "down", and help us keep our balance. An unpowered spaceship is actually in free fall, with the ship and the astronauts falling together in a condition of apparent **WEIGHTLESSNESS**. The astronauts' semicircular canals can't tell which direction is "down", which causes "space sickness".

WHO DOES THE MOST WORK ON A TANDEM?

The amount of effort needed to move the tandem **FORWARDS** is the same front and back. If both riders have equal ability and make an equal effort, they'll each contribute **50 PER CENT** of the effort needed to move the bike forward. However, the rider in the back seat can easily get away with putting in less effort, since the person at the front **CAN'T SEE** what the person behind is doing!

How do tightrope walkers keep their balance?

Tightrope walkers often carry a **LONG FLEXIBLE POLE**, the ends of which droop below the tightrope. This moves the **CENTRE OF GRAVITY** of the walker and pole closer to the tightrope, which makes it easier to balance. The long pole also helps counteract any **WOBBLINESS** before falling.

If DIAMONDS are the hardest substance, how do jewellers cut them?

They use DIAMONDS. Until recently, there were two main ways to cut diamonds. One was to find a WEAK SPOT in the jewel and split it there using a small hammer and chisel. The other was to use a DIAMOND-EDGED blade. Today, jewellers use a small saw coated in diamond dust or a hi-tech laser.

WHY DO NEW TRAINERS SQUEAK ON A GYM FLOOR?

The sound comes from the **RUBBER** soles sticking to the smooth floor, snapping off, and then sticking again straight away. This happens over and over again very quickly, making the rubber vibrate, which makes the air vibrate – **SCREECH!** Dragging a finger around a wet wine glass rim creates sound in a similar way.

Why does wet stuff feel cold?

Two reasons. Water loses heat as it **EVAPORATES**, making it cold. It also conducts (takes) heat away from your skin very quickly.

Why is there iodine in my salt?

A) It makes **SALT** taste salty.

B) IODINE and salt are the same thing.

C) It is put there to **KEEP YOU HEALTHY**.

WHY DOES SOME SOAP LATHER MORE THAN OTHERS?

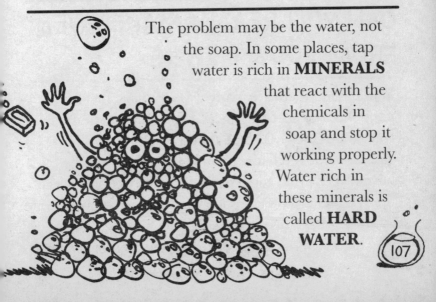

The problem may be the water, not the soap. In some places, tap water is rich in **MINERALS** that react with the chemicals in soap and stop it working properly. Water rich in these minerals is called **HARD WATER**.

Where do the stripes in toothpaste come from?

A) The toothpaste tube contains a long **WINDING** channel with stripes running all the way through.

B) A coloured **DYE** is added as the toothpaste comes out.

C) The **FRONT** and **BACK** of the tube contain different-coloured pastes.

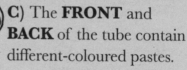

Answer: (C) The rear of the tube contains white toothpaste and the front contains coloured toothpaste. The nozzle is connected to the rear by a cylindrical pipe that also has four small holes near the front. When you squeeze, white paste is forced along the pipe and coloured paste is forced into the four small holes, making stripes.

CAN YOU REALLY MAKE FUEL FROM POO?

Yep. In fact, there are many ways to make fuel from poo. One way is to put sewage in a huge vat and then collect the smelly **GASES** that seep out of it. These gases include methane (natural gas), which can be burned as fuel. In some parts of world, people collect the **DUNG** of cows or other plant-eating animals after it has dried in the sun. The fibrous plant matter in the dung makes a good fuel for bonfires.

Why doesn't wood melt?

Wood **BURNS** before it gets a chance to melt. The fire is the result of a **CHEMICAL REACTION** between energy-rich carbon compounds in wood and oxygen in the air. The energy is released as heat and light, forming flames. If you heated wood inside a vacuum (a space containing no air), the carbon within it would eventually melt at 3,500°C (6,330°F).

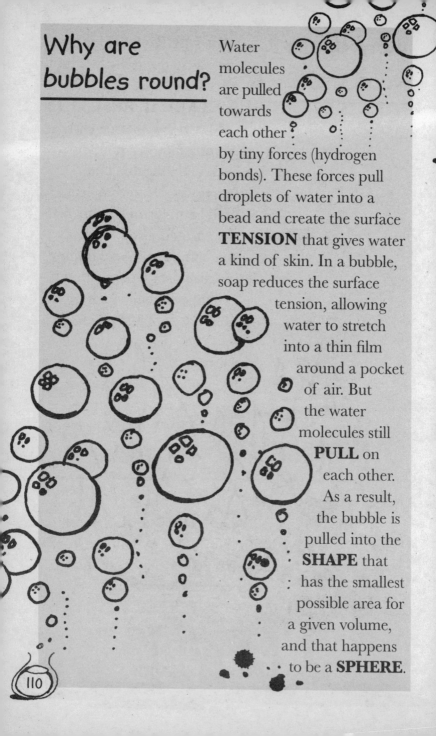

Why are bubbles round?

Water molecules are pulled towards each other by tiny forces (hydrogen bonds). These forces pull droplets of water into a bead and create the surface **TENSION** that gives water a kind of skin. In a bubble, soap reduces the surface tension, allowing water to stretch into a thin film around a pocket of air. But the water molecules still **PULL** on each other. As a result, the bubble is pulled into the **SHAPE** that has the smallest possible area for a given volume, and that happens to be a **SPHERE**.

WHY IS JUICE STICKY WHEN YOU SPILL IT, BUT NOT WHEN YOU DRINK IT?

The **STICKINESS** comes from sugar, which is what makes syrup and honey so sticky. Juice contains sugar but a lot of **WATER**. If you spill it, the water **EVAPORATES** and the sugar becomes concentrated. The more concentrated the sugar, the stickier the puddle.

Why does a metal bench make my bum colder than a wooden one?

Metal is a better **CONDUCTOR** of heat than wood. When you sit on a metal bench, it conducts (takes) the heat from your body **FASTER** than a wooden bench does, which makes your skin **COLDER.**

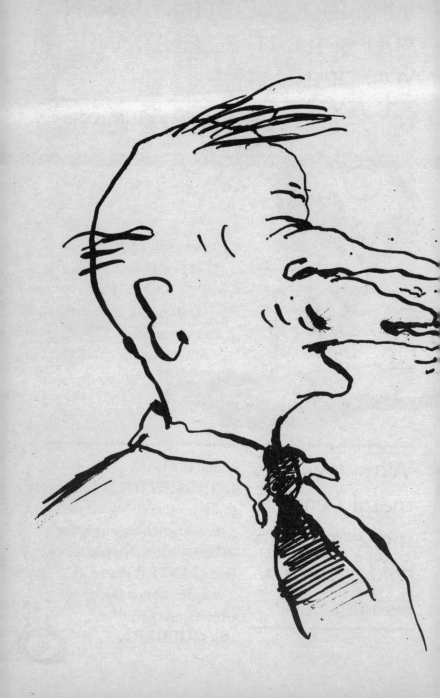

SAVOUR THE FLAVOUR

It's a taste sensation!

Why does PEPPER make you SNEEZE?

You SNEEZE because your nose is trying to get rid of the pepper it has accidentally hoovered up. Pepper contains a chemical called PIPERINE that really gets up your nose by irritating the nerve endings inside the mucous membrane (the bit that produces snot). Your nose reacts to the irritation by blasting the pepper out at 160 km/h (100 mph).

What makes bread rise?

A) FARTING fungi.

B) Anti-gravity **FLOUR**.

C) It has ambitions to go **UP** in the world.

Answer: (A) The yeast used to make bread is a type of fungus. It feeds on the sugars in flour and gives off gas. As the bread bakes, this gas expands, giving bread an airy, fluffy texture.

Do mints really make your mouth cold?

No – a mint just makes your mouth **FEEL** as if it's cold. The minty taste comes from a chemical called **MENTHOL**. The menthol sensitizes nerve cells in your mouth that sense cold and tricks your brain into thinking you're eating something cool. But the temperature in your mouth has not changed at all.

WHY DO CHILLIES MAKE YOUR MOUTH FEEL LIKE IT'S BURNING?

Chillies work in much the same way as mints, only the chemical in chillies, **CAPSAICIN**, tricks your brain into thinking your mouth is getting hotter. Different peppers contain different amounts of capsaicin, which is why some peppers make your mouth feel only a little hot, while others make you feel like you're on **FIRE**.

Why does garlic make your breath smell?

A) It makes your **MOUTH** produce anti-vampire gases.

B) Garlic contains a lot of **SMELLY** chemicals.

C) Because it clings to your **TEETH**.

Answer: (B) Garlic contains a smelly chemical called allicin. Allicin contains sulphur – the same substance that makes rotten eggs smell horrible. But some of the other chemicals in garlic help the bacteria that live naturally in your mouth grow better. More bacteria mean more bad breath.

Why does warm milk make you feel sleepy?

A) The milk contains a **CHEMICAL** that acts like a natural sleeping pill.

B) The warmth **LULLS** you to sleep.

C) It reminds your body of when you were a **BABY** and took lots of naps.

Answer: (A) Milk contains a natural chemical called tryptophan, which stimulates the production of a chemical in the brain that makes people feel calm. The temperature of the milk makes no difference to the effect of the tryptophan.

WHY DOES ASPARAGUS MAKE YOUR PEE SMELL?

Asparagus is notorious for producing **PUNGENT** sulphur compounds that end up in your urine after you've eaten it. However, studies suggest that your body's ability to make these compounds depends on your **GENES** – some people don't produce smelly urine after eating the stuff. Genetics might also be affecting your ability to smell these compounds – not everyone who excretes them can smell them.

Does eating carrots really help you see in the dark?

Well, have you ever seen a rabbit with night-vision goggles? Seriously, carrots are a good source of **VITAMIN A** (which is important for healthy eyes), but eating them by the bucketload doesn't make your eyesight any better. This myth started in World War II because the British air ministry didn't want the Germans to know they had invented **RADAR**. So they spread the rumour that British pilots were good at shooting down German planes at night because they were eating plenty of carrots.

WHY DOES STALE BREAD TURN HARD, BUT STALE BISCUITS TURN SOFT?

Biscuits turn **SOFT** because they have a lot more sugar and salt than bread. Sugar and salt soak up **WATER** from the air. Bread has a lot of flour, which does not absorb moisture from the air. Instead, bread **LOSES MOISTURE** to the air and becomes hard.

What should you drink after eating spicy food to put out the fire in your mouth?

A) **WATER**.

B) **MILK**.

C) **JUICE**.

Answer: (B) Milk is probably best out of these because it contains some fat. The capsaicin that makes your mouth burn is a bit oily, so a watery drink is not a good idea as oil and water don't mix, but the fats in the milk will. The best way to put out the fire is to eat a bit of bread or rice, as this will wipe the capsaicin oil off the surface of your mouth.

Why does popcorn pop?

A) It likes **SCARING** people who want to eat it.

B) It's the noise it makes when it **EXPLODES** as it's being heated.

C) It's trying to **ESCAPE** from the heat of the pan.

Answer: (B) Popcorn kernels contain water. As the kernel is heated, the water turns to steam and pressure builds up in the kernel. Eventually, the seed covering breaks and the inside of the kernel (which is mostly made of starch) expands to form a fluffy, white piece of popcorn.

WHERE DO THE HOLES COME FROM IN SWISS CHEESE?

They're made by **BACTERIA** burping as they turn the milk into cheese. During this process the bacteria eat a substance in milk called **LACTIC** acid and give out large amounts of carbon dioxide gas. The gas collects in big bubbles before the cheese hardens.

Can you DIG to the other side of the WORLD?

Put down your shovels – it's never going to work! Before long, the heat and pressure would make it impossible to keep going. If you managed to dig down 60 km (37 miles) or so, you'd reach the outer mantle, where the rock reaches temperatures of nearly 1,000°C (1,800°F). If you kept going to the planet's iron inner core, the temperature would soar to 4,700°C (8,500°F). And even if you could survive the heat, you'd still be crushed by the pressure.

HOW MUCH WATER IS THERE ON EARTH?

A whole lot! There are about **369 MILLION TRILLION GALLONS** of water on Earth. If all that water was poured into a balloon, the balloon would measure about one-third of the diameter of the Moon. About 98% of Earth's water is salt water, and most of the rest is frozen fresh water trapped in the ice caps of the North and South Poles.

Why is the sea salty?

A) Many years ago, a meteor made of **SALT** crashed into the Pacific Ocean.

B) RIVERS have washed the salt off the land.

C) The salt comes from millions of **DEAD FISH**.

Answer: (B) The ground beneath our feet contains many different kinds of minerals. As water flows downhill, it dissolves minerals and washes them into the ocean. Over time this has made the sea salty.

What is the best way to escape from quicksand?

The key is not to **PANIC**. If you make sudden flailing movements, the quicksand will get thicker and you'll pull yourself further in. Whatever you do, don't let other people try to pull you out when you're deep in the sand, because you could be seriously injured! The best solution is to make small, **GENTLE** movements to loosen the sand. As your body comes up to the surface, just lie back and float. Then your friends can help get you out.

WHAT IS OIL MADE FROM?

Oil is made from squashed-up, ancient **DEAD STUFF**. Tiny life forms called plankton and algae lived in the seas millions of years ago. Some of these sank to the bottom of the ocean when they died, and were covered over by sand or mud. Without the oxygen needed for normal rotting, they turned into a kind of fossil called **KEROGEN**. Over millions of years, more and more layers of sediment covered over the kerogen, and the pressure and heat from this crushing weight transformed it into oil.

Why can't we see the air?

Air is made up of a mixture of nitrogen, oxygen, water vapour, carbon dioxide and argon. Fortunately for us, these gases hardly absorb or reflect any visible light. But if you cool oxygen into a liquid, it turns a **VIVID BLUE** colour!

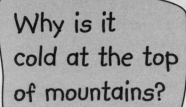

Why is it cold at the top of mountains?

A) Air cools as it gets more spread out. So the **THIN AIR** at the top of mountains is especially chilly.

B) Because it's closer to **SPACE**, and space is incredibly cold.

C) The **SNOW** on the mountains cools the air.

Answer: (A) As you get higher, the air gets thinner – there's just less of it around. That's why mountaineers sometimes use oxygen masks. Air is a gas, and like all gases it cools as it expands. The taller the mountain, the colder the air will be.

WHAT IS THE LOWEST POINT ON EARTH?

That depends on whether you want to get wet! The Krubera Cave in Georgia is 2,191 metres (7,188 feet) below sea level. Whereas the lowest point is the bottom of the Mariana Trench in the Pacific Ocean, which is nearly 11 km (6.8 miles) below sea level.

Where's the best place to hide during an earthquake?

The best place to be during an earthquake is on a plane! But if you're on the ground, it depends on whether you're indoors or outdoors. If you're in a building, get under a load-bearing door frame or under a sturdy table away from any windows. If you're outdoors, make your way to an open space far from any buildings, power lines, or trees.

WHY DOESN'T EVERYTHING FLY INTO SPACE?

GRAVITY is just too strong to let the spinning Earth fling objects away from it. But did you know that you weigh less at the **EQUATOR**, where the Earth is spinning fastest, than you do at the poles?

Why is the sky blue?

Light travels in waves like ripples on a pond, and each colour we see is a light wave of a different **LENGTH**. White light from the Sun is a mixture of light of every colour. The longer waves that make up red, orange, and yellow light pass straight through air molecules. However, the shorter, **BLUE WAVES** are absorbed by the molecules in the air, and are scattered all around the sky. So when you look up into the sky, it's the scattered blue light you see.

INDEX